RAINBOW OF ANIMALS

WHY ARE ANIMALS BLUE?

Melissa Stewart

Series Literacy Consultant:
Allan A. De Fina, Ph.D.
Past President of the New Jersey Reading Association
Dean, College of Education
New Jersey City University, Jersey City, NJ

Series Science Consultant:
Helen Hess, Ph.D.
Professor of Biology
College of the Atlantic
Bar Harbor, Maine

Contents

Words to Know

attract (uh TRAKT)—To make interested.

poison (POY zuhn)—Something that can make an animal sick. Sometimes the animal gets so sick that it dies.

predator (PREH duh tur)—An animal that hunts and kills other animals for food.

prey (PRAY)—An animal that is hunted by a predator.

northern
cardinal

yellow boxfish

A Rainbow of Animals

panther chameleon

poison dart
frog

Go outside and look around. How many kinds of animals do you see? Birds and fish are animals. So are spiders and insects. Animals come in all sizes and shapes. And they come in all the colors of the rainbow.

leaf-mimic katydid

lesser purple
emperor butterfly

Blue Animals Near You

Can you think of some blue animals that live near you? Some birds are blue. So are some insects.

Blue animals live in other parts of the world, too. Let's take a look at some of them.

Blue Shark

Being blue helps some animals hide. This shark's blue body makes it hard to see as it swims through the ocean. That helps the hungry hunter sneak up on its **prey**.

Blue-Ringed Octopus

This animal's pale skin and blue rings make it stand out. When enemies see these bright colors, they know to stay away.

It would be a bad idea to attack this octopus. Its body has enough **poison** to kill twenty people.